40

PRAYERS

FOR ADVENT

**Prayers for your
Church or small group**

DAVID CLOWES

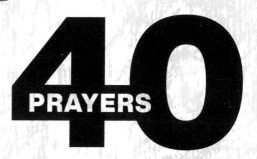

DAVID **C** COOK

transforming lives together

40 PRAYERS FOR ADVENT
Published by David C Cook
4050 Lee Vance Drive
Colorado Springs, CO 80918 U.S.A.

Integrity Music Limited, a Division of David C Cook
Brighton, East Sussex BN1 2RE, England

The website addresses recommended throughout this book
are offered as a resource to you. These websites are not
intended in any way to be or imply an endorsement on the
part of David C Cook, nor do we vouch for their content.

ISBN 978-0-8307-8230-7
eISBN 978-0-8307-8238-3

© 2020 David Clowes

The Team: Ian Matthews, Jack Campbell,
Jo Stockdale, Susan Murdock

Cover Design: Pete Barnsley

Printed in the United Kingdom
First Edition 2020

1 2 3 4 5 6 7 8 9 10

090120

40 PRAYERS

FOR ADVENT

CONTENTS

INTRODUCTION

Having published *500 Prayers for All Occasions* and *500 More Prayers for All Occasions* I was asked to develop a new series of books of prayer for use in small groups or in the home.

There are at least forty prayers in each of these books based around a single theme. Most of the content comes from my first two books of prayer for public worship, but has been revised and re-worked to make them appropriate for use in churches, small groups, the family situation, or for personal quiet time devotions.

My church background was firmly in the camp of extemporary prayer. I started to write my prayers down due to nervousness and on the advice of my preaching mentor who insisted on careful preparation not only of the hymns, readings, and sermon, but also of the prayers. I have long since realised the value of having a resource to be used as a flexible launch pad for my own prayer life which I could use and adapt as I wished.

I hope that is how you will approach these simple aids to prayer. They have been deliberately written in an uncomplicated style and with language that seeks to illuminate the joy of prayer. I have also tried to ensure that they are written in the language we use in our daily conversations. The aim of this is designed to make them easier to 'pray' and not simply to 'read'.

David Clowes
Stockport, April 2020

PRAYERS OF APPROACH

THE LORD IS HERE

The Lord is here, and we will praise him.
The Lord is here, and we will worship him.
The Lord is here, and we will trust him.
The Lord is here, and we will honour him.
The Lord is here,
and he has called us to give him all the glory. **Amen.**

HIS NAME

His name is Almighty
and he is the Lord.
His name is Creator
and he makes all things new.
His name is Sustainer
and he holds us in the palm of his hand.
His name is Saviour
and he died in our place.

His name is Forgiveness
and he can be trusted to heal and to bless.
His name is Holy
and he is the one that we have come to worship.
His name means
he is worthy to receive all we have and all we are.
Amen.

THE WORD OF GOD

Lord, we have heard of all that you have done
in and through the lives of your people—
down the centuries and across the world.
You have touched and changed people's whole way
of living;
you have made people new.
We have come to worship you,
to be changed by you,
to become the people you always meant us to be.
Let it happen, Lord, even though we are afraid of
change
and resist any alteration of our way of life.
Challenge us and change us and fill us
with such an awareness of you and your presence
that nothing,
not even our own hearts and lives,
can ever be the same again. **Amen.**

A WORLD OF CHANGE

Lord, we live in a world of change.
Every day is filled with uncertainty.
We are surrounded by the twists and turns of life
and we often feel we have little or no control over
    things that happen to us.
Lord, we come to stand in your eternal presence.
We come to you to find ourselves.
We come to you to find our way.
We come to you to find hope.
We come to you because in Christ you first came
    to us. **Amen.**

NOTHING TO PROVE

Father, we do not come to prove our own worth
    to you,
or to be accepted because of our good deeds
or the greatness of our faith.
We come simply as we are: small, sinful, and weak.
We come trusting in your mercy
and daring to believe that you can and will
    accomplish greater things in our lives
than we can ask or think.
We come in the name of Christ
to worship you for your glory, power, and love.
    Amen.

THE ANNUNCIATION

Father, we come with our hurts, our sorrows, and
our uncertainties.
We come to hold on to your promises of healing and
hope.
We come to be held by you
and to prepare for the coming of Christ as Saviour
to change the world and renew our lives.
We also come to allow Christ to prepare us for his
coming again as Lord,
when we shall praise him and laugh and sing and
worship for ever. **Amen.**

PRAYERS OF PRAISE

YOU DO NOT CHANGE

Lord, you do not change; you are always there and
   you always will be.
We praise you for your greatness which holds our
   smallness;
for your majesty which was once clothed with our
   humanity;
for your sovereignty which embraces our frailty;
for your holiness which exposes our sinfulness;
for your wholeness which heals our brokenness;
for your glory which fills our emptiness;
for your love that gives us life;
for your Son who claims us for his own;
for your Spirit who empowers us for worship,
   witness, and service.
Wonderful God, Lord of all time and space and
   all things,
we praise you that in Christ you came

and shared all that life means to us so that we, by
    your grace,
might enter into all that heaven is with him.
We have come to praise you for the coming of
    Christ our Saviour
and the Saviour of the world.
In his name. **Amen.**

AMAZING GOD

Amazing God! We praise you, the living God.
We praise you, the God who is alive and the God
    who gives us life.
We praise you for your acts for and on behalf of your
    people
down the centuries and across the world.
We praise you today for the record of all you have
    said and done in the Scriptures;
for all we can learn of you through the work of the
    Holy Spirit upon the pages of the Bible.
We praise you for the truth we have received about
    Jesus Christ
and his knowledge and love of the Scriptures.
We praise you for the way they guided his life and
    ministry as your uniquely precious Son.
We praise you more that he has become the very
    focal point for every part of our lives.
We praise you for the fulfilment of Scripture in him.

In his life, death, and resurrection he gathered up
    and completed
all that, down the centuries, you had promised.
We praise you for the assurance in him
that no matter the trials and problems we face today,
we, like him, will share in your promise
of the ultimate victory of your purposes for all
    your creation.
In the name of him whose life and presence fulfils
    your Word. **Amen.**

YOU ARE THERE

Father, we praise you that whoever we are and
    wherever we go, you are there.
We have discovered that there is simply nowhere we
    can go where you will not be present.
We cannot hide, we cannot run, we cannot even be
    there before you!
We praise you that you are always ahead of us,
    preparing the way.
You are there waiting with arms of love and mercy
to hold us and to welcome us,
to heal us and to hold us.
Lord, you are ever near, ever approachable.
In the midst of our anxiety and fear
you are always understanding, coming into our
    turmoil, our doubts,

our weakness and despair, and you come with peace.
You stand guard over our hearts and minds
so that we dare to speak your name and serve your
     kingdom.
Great and wonderful God, always loving, we praise
     and honour you.
Your majesty is beyond our reach,
your fatherly love so gentle and accepting is
     always near.
We praise you for your love and truth made known
     in the word of the prophets,
in your word made flesh in Jesus;
in his dying and his rising.
We praise you here and will praise you everywhere.
We praise you now and will praise you for ever.
   Amen.

WONDERFUL GOD

Wonderful God! You are almighty, all-powerful,
     and all-loving.
We praise you, our creator God,
who has given us eyes to see the signs of your
     handiwork.
All around us we recognise your fingerprints:
in the grandeur of hills and mountains and in
     mighty oceans and rivers;
in the intricate beauty of a flower;
in the healing, caring touch of a friend;

in the innocent smile of a child;
in the courage of those who struggle against the odds;
in the fellowship of your people everywhere.
We praise you for Jesus Christ, your Son,
the human sign of your presence
and the proof that you are among us as Saviour.
We praise you, not only that he came,
but also for the way he came:
born as one of us;
sharing our lives and our limitations
of time and space;
facing all the pressures and temptations that came
    from living in a fallen world.
We praise you for the Holy Spirit at work in his birth,
    life, and ministry.
We praise you for his death and resurrection
and the promise of the Spirit for all your people.
Here and now, we celebrate the victory of your love
    that will never be defeated
but will conquer all that spoils your world and
    our lives.
We will praise you here and everywhere, now and
    for ever. **Amen.**

WE'VE BEEN MEANING TO SAY

Lord, we've been meaning to say
something of how hard we are finding it
to trust you, to pray, to walk the path of discipleship.

Lord, we've been meaning to say
that so often we feel we are walking alone,
that no one else sees things the way we do.
We know deep inside that we have so much
    to share,
so much good news to give,
but it appears that no one wants to listen
    anymore.

Lord, we've been meaning to say
how disillusioned we are becoming;
we feel a dryness within that we have never
    experienced before
and each day we are finding it harder
to find a way out of our prison of emptiness.

Lord, we've been meaning to say
that we always thought we could rely on you
to make sure that nothing really awful ever
    happened to us;
that nothing would challenge our faith
or make the way you are leading us seem so dark
    and uncertain.

Lord, we've been meaning to say
that our world has changed.
The picture we once held in our minds of you
    and your power and your love

has been torn from our grasp.
It seems that the time has come when we are
    having to learn all over again
to walk by faith and not by sight;
to trust you, even when the darkness is
    deepest;
to believe that you will keep your promise—
to be there for us in ways too deep for words.

Lord, we've been meaning to say
though we have treated this world as if it were
    our own,
in this Advent moment, we are preparing to
    watch you step
into a world which is yours and which your
    love has created,
though we have treated it as if it were our own.
Once more you will remind us that you are
the alpha and the omega, the beginning and
    the end.
You who had the first word will most certainly
    have the last.
This is your promise and this is our hope.
By the Holy Spirit, hold our hand, guide us
    through the darkness
to your glorious, overwhelming light
and into the peace that only you can give.
In Christ's name. **Amen.**

WHAT SHALL WE CALL HIM?

wonderful	—	forgiving;
beautiful	—	creative;
holy	—	overwhelming;
merciful	—	patient;
gracious	—	understanding;
loving	—	trusting;
incarnate	—	eternal;
crucified	—	risen;
all-powerful	—	gentle;
all-knowing	—	faithful.

Almighty, King of creation, sovereign over all things.
We can't find the right words
when all we long to say is
you are our Saviour and you are our Lord,
and we will adore you. **Amen.**

THE PROMISE OF FREEDOM

Father, we thank you for all your faithful people
who, like Moses, have come with words of hope,
    faith, and love
and who have acted with courage, patience, and
    openness to set people free;
for all those who have touched our lives with
    their lives
and whose words and deeds have spoken to us
    of Christ;

for those who have challenged our way of life
and drawn us closer to the one who makes all
   things new;
for all your faithful people down the centuries
whose words and deeds have changed history;
for those who, through the Holy Spirit,
have power to transform lives today.
We thank you for all who have acted with courage
to set people free from injustice, oppression, and all
   that spoils life.
We praise you that through the Spirit of Christ we
   can be free
to worship you in truth, to serve you in love,
and to witness to your praise and glory.
Lord, may our words and our thoughts and our lives
enable others to enter your freedom in Christ.
   Amen.

PRAYERS OF THANKSGIVING

THANK YOU FOR THE HOPE

Father, we thank you for the hope with which you
     have filled our lives.
We give thanks that in the coming of Christ
you have given us assurance of your sovereign
     control of all things.
Thank you for this Advent Sunday when we remember
not only the coming of Christ to be the Saviour
     of the world
but also the promise of his coming again as Lord of all.
Thank you for the hope with which Christ fills
     our lives.
In our times of doubt and despair, the message of his
     coming,
his birth, life, death, and resurrection, reassures us
     and renews our hope.
Thank you that because of Christ's coming and the
     promise of his coming again

we can live each day to the full in the knowledge
 that you are with us
and that ultimately you hold all things,
including ourselves, in your mercy, love, and care.
Lord, come, and come again.
Come into your world.
Come into our lives that we might have hope.
In Jesus' name. **Amen.**

YOUR WORD OF TRUTH

Lord, we give you thanks for the truth of your Word.
So many have promised so much to so many people
 for so long.
But we have found that your Word is to be trusted.
Thank you for the stories of men and women
who were chosen and called by you and who
 served you.
When they failed, you restored them and
 forgave them.
Thank you for all who have listened to your Word
and sought to enable others to hear it too.
We thank you for all teachers and preachers and for
 biblical scholars
who have brought the meaning and the joy of the
 Bible alive for us today.
Thank you that your word in the Bible is still alive
 and active
to keep us calm and strong and full of hope.

Thank you that the Bible is not simply a book of
    things that happened long ago,
but that you still speak to people today through your
    Word.
Thank you for those moments when we have been
    very much aware
of your word for us at particular times in our lives.
When we were sad, you comforted us;
when we were wayward, you warned us;
when we wandered off on our own way, you called
    us back to yourself;
when we were lost, you spoke and led us home;
when we were afraid, you gave us hope;
when we thought we knew best, you waited
    patiently and loved us still;
when we were hurting and there was no one to help
    us, you came and held us in your arms.
Thank you, Lord, for being there
when no one else wanted to or could be.
Thank you that Jesus is always your word of hope
    to us. **Amen.**

TO KNOW YOU ARE REAL

Almighty God, our heavenly Father,
we thank you for men and women who, like John
    the Baptist,
have made it possible for others to hear you speak,

to know you are real, and to make ready to welcome
     you into their lives.
We thank you for those who have been ready to
     stand and be counted,
to suffer loss and rejection rather than deny the truth
     of Christ within them.
Thank you for those today, even in our materialistic
     society,
whose words and deeds demonstrate the reality of
     your presence;
those whose way of life gives hope to others and
     glory to you
as their lives reaffirm your extravagant love.
Father, we thank you for those whose deeds opened
     our eyes to your truth,
whose words opened our ears to your voice,
whose lives opened our hearts to the power of
     the Spirit.
We thank you for those who made Christ real;
for those who made us hungry for his love and
     thirsty for his refreshing joy.
May we, by your Holy Spirit,
be a channel of your life-refreshing, life transforming
     grace for others.
In the name of Christ, our Lord. **Amen.**

EXTRAVAGANT LOVE

Lord, how can we not thank you for your
  extravagant love to us in Christ?
We thank you for the way you have made yourself
  and your purposes known—
not to the high and mighty
but to those who knew they were unworthy
and had done nothing to deserve your love.
We thank you for the way you constantly surprise us
by coming to us when we least expect it;
you open our hearts and minds and lives to the truth
  of your presence and power.
Thank you for your coming to Mary to surprise her
  with joy and understanding.
Thank you that knowing you and being
part of your purposes never depends on our age or
  our achievements
but entirely upon your grace.
Thank you for the story of Mary
and for the assurance and challenge it brings of the
  width of your love
and the irresistible power of your glory.
Make us, we pray, channels of your surprising grace
  today.
In the name of the one who came and comes and
  calls. **Amen.**

PRAYERS OF CONFESSION

FORGIVE US

Lord, forgive us our daily acts of faithlessness,
the anxieties that cripple our lives,
and the sense of hopelessness that hinders our
    growth.
Forgive us our fear which prevents us from speaking
    out
or from telling the good news of Jesus.
Forgive us our weakness which causes us to let you
    down
and our bitterness which makes it harder for others
    to find you.
Forgive us our hard-heartedness which crushes hope
    for our neighbour
and our self-centredness which causes you pain.
Take hold of our lives all over again.

Make us a source of hope, joy, and confidence
for those who need our faithfulness,
and, by your Spirit, enable us to be beacons of your
     light and love. **Amen.**

YOUR WORD

Forgive us, Father, that though we possess the Bible,
     we rarely read it.
Forgive us that though we read it, we rarely think
     about what you have told us.
Forgive us that even when we have pondered your
     Word, we rarely put what you have said into
     practice.
Father, forgive us that we resist your will and word
     for us:
 the challenge to love our neighbour and ourselves;
 the call to speak a word of hope and comfort;
 the commission to speak out against evil;
 and to call others to follow Christ.
 Forgive us.
 Awaken us all over again
 to find delight in reading your Word,
 pondering its meaning for today
 and allowing the Spirit to bring the word
 that heals and restores to our lost and hurting world.
 Through Christ, the Word of God. **Amen.**

WE STAND IN YOUR PRESENCE

Lord, when we stand in your presence,
all our pride and self-sufficiency, our self-interest and
    self-satisfaction
are exposed as the self-delusions they are.
Lord, when you come to us,
our superstitions, our lies, our half-truths, and our
    self-deceit crumble like dust before you.
The selfish way we make use of one another,
the way we look down in contempt on other people,
our vanity and our self-righteousness
are shown up in all their poverty and emptiness.
Father, we seek your forgiveness and resist your
    life-renewing Spirit no longer.
Lift us up and enable us to celebrate your love made
    known to us in the risen Christ. **Amen.**

COUNTING THE COST

Forgive us, Lord, when we do count the cost and
    find that the price is too high;
when we know that you are calling us but we don't
    want to listen;
when you challenge us to trust you but we would
    rather put our faith in ourselves;
when we know we should pray but we have left you
    no time;
when your word is before us but we are afraid you
    will speak;

when you tell us to keep no score of wrongs, but we
    keep writing the list;
when you teach us to pray 'forgive us as we forgive
    others'
but the truth is we don't really mean it!
Yet we need to know that we are accepted, loved,
    and forgiven.
By your grace, transform what we are,
and by your Holy Spirit may we live for your glory.
    Amen.

PRAYERS FOR ALL-AGE WORSHIP

YOU ARE NOT REMOTE

Heavenly Father,
we praise you that you have shown us in Jesus
that you are not remote and you are not a long way
    from us.
Though we cannot see you or touch you,
you have promised that no matter who or what
    we are,
what we have done or failed to do,
you will be very near to each and every one of us.

As we prepare for Christmas,
the time when we shall remember the coming
    of Jesus,
help us to know, really to know, the joy of his living
    presence in our lives.
Father, we praise you that he came, just as we did,
    as a helpless baby.

His coming has left us in no doubt as to the love and
    mercy you are offering to us.
We praise you that in and through Jesus
you have already opened the way to real life now
and to life with you for all eternity.
Father, we praise you for all those who,
by their faith in you and their faithfulness to you,
have prepared the way for your love
to reach out into the world and into our lives.
    Amen.

STORIES

We praise you for all the stories in the Bible
that tell us of your goodness towards us
and your love for the whole world.
We praise you for the story of Mary and Joseph,
the shepherds and the angels, the wise men and the
    star.
We praise you for the carols we sing
and the joy we share in celebrating the coming of
    your Son.

We praise you more that it is all not just a story
but a message that tells of the birth of the Saviour of
    the world,
the one who is coming to open the way back to you,
for all who will open their lives to him.

We praise you that Jesus has promised
that no matter what we are facing,
whether it brings pain or pleasure,
joy or sorrow, despair or hope,
whether in the rush or in the stillness,
in times of noise or in the quiet moments of life,
he is Immanuel; he will be with us. **Amen.**

TEACH US TO REMEMBER

Father, teach us to remember he is the one
    who came,
he is the one who comes, and he is the one who
    will come again.
Forgive us if we spend so much time preparing to
    enjoy ourselves,
that we forget those who will have no joy this
    Christmas.
Forgive us that as we decorate our homes,
we forget those who have no home.
Forgive us if, as we welcome the baby in the manger,
we forget he is the man on the cross.
Forgive us if, in all our preparations,
we fail to make time and space in our Christmas
    for you.
We ask our prayer in the name of Jesus,
who came that we might have life—life in all its
    fullness. **Amen.**

WE DON'T NEED TO PRETEND

Father, we thank you that we can come into your
    presence just as we are.
We do not have to pretend to be good and kind
    and helpful
because you know what we are really like.
You know just how easy we find it
to be selfish, unkind, and to want our own way.
You know how hard we find it to like other people,
and that to love them is even harder.

We thank you for helping us to see something
of your tremendous love towards us
and for your understanding of the difficulties we face
    every day.
We thank you that in Jesus you shared all our
    experiences of life.
In him you added the experience of what it means
    to be us
to your knowledge of what it means to be God.
We praise you that there is nothing
that hurts us or makes us sad or afraid that you do
    not understand.

There is no fear, doubt, or worry that you do
    not know.
You know what it means to feel rejected, unwanted,
    and unloved.

You know how it feels when your friends do not
    want you
and you feel as if you are on your own.

Jesus has given us hope of his coming to live in our
    hearts and lives.
We have the assurance that he will be with us when
    no one else wants to be there
and no one else can be there.
Forgive us for not showing your love to one another
and for our failure to stand by our friends in
    their need.
Fill us with the love of Jesus. **Amen.**

YOUR WORD

Lord, we thank you not only for loving us
but also for telling us of your love.
We thank you that you not only told us of your love
but you also showed it to us in Jesus.
We thank you that the Bible tells us that you made
    the world,
and for scientists who are discovering how it
    was made.

We thank you for the stories of all you did for
    your people;
for leaders like Moses, Abraham, and Elijah

and for those who wrote the Psalms to your praise.
We thank you for Jesus and his stories
and teaching about you and your kingdom;
for his acts of love and kindness
that brought healing and sight to those in need.
We thank you that he is not just a name in the Bible
or simply a man who lived and died a long time ago.
Through your Holy Spirit we can know Jesus in our
lives today.
Forgive us that we close our ears to your call
to love our neighbour as ourselves.
Touch us and change us and make us new.
In Jesus' name. **Amen.**

GOOD THINGS

Father, we thank you that we can call you Father
and for all the good things which make each day so
exciting;
for the different things we can see and hear and taste
and touch.
We thank you for those who add so many good
things to our lives;
for those who help us when we are in need
and those who find us when we feel lost.
Thank you for those whose kindness and friendship
make life worthwhile
and for those who love us even when we are not very
nice to know.

You have made us so that we can know you and your
 love for us
and that this love comes to us in Jesus.
We praise you that he loved us so much
that though he belonged with you in heaven,
he continued to live the life of a human being
and died for us in our place,
 and you raised him to life
so that he might live in our hearts.
Thank you for those who have told us about Jesus
and for those whose lives make him real.
We pray that we might live for him each day
that others might know your love too. **Amen.**

IT'S ADVENT

Advent
We pray for those who are Angry and for those who
 are Alone;
for those who have been Abused by others;
and for those who Ache to be Accepted.
May the coming of Jesus fill them with hope.

aDvent
We pray for those who feel Defeated by all that they
 face each day;
for those who are sick or Dying;
and for those who are filled with Despair.
May the coming of Jesus fill them with hope.

adVent

We pray for those with a Vision for peace
and for those who are the Voice of the poor;
for those who teach us to Value one another;
and for those who work with the Vulnerable, the
    homeless, and the lost.
May the coming of Jesus fill them with hope.

advEnt

We pray for planet Earth and for those who
    Encourage us to care for it;
for those seeking to Escape the fighting in
    [*name a country*];
and for those working to provide
Essential food and clothing for the world's refugees.
May the coming of Jesus fill them with hope.

adveNt

We pray for our Neighbours—
those who live next door, across the road,
    or across the world;
for those who are seeking to follow the Narrow way;
and for those who Name the name of Jesus
and bring good News of him to others.
May the coming of Jesus fill them with hope.

*adven**T***

We pray for those whose lives have been changed by
the work of Terrorists;

for those whose faith has been Tested by the things
that have happened to them;

for those who Teach us about Jesus;

and for those who should be the Target of our love.

May the coming of Jesus fill them with hope.

We ask our prayers in the name of Jesus,

the one who comes with hope. **Amen.**

PRAYERS FOR INTERCESSIONS

THINK OF SOMEONE

Think of someone whose life is in turmoil,
who is facing a time of change and who is not sure
which way to go or where to find help or how to
    cope with tomorrow.
Ask that Christ's coming may fill them
    with strength.

Think of someone who is struggling
to cope with the onset of illness or old age
and looks back to unfulfilled dreams and
    broken promises.
Ask that Christ's coming may fill them with hope.

Think of someone who is overwhelmed
by the pressures and the responsibilities laid
    upon them;

someone for whom the expectations of parents,
    employers, society, or themselves
are becoming too much to bear.
Ask that Christ's coming may fill them with a sense
    of their own worth.

Think of someone who is facing the implications of
    the wrong decisions they have made;
those who have made money, financial success or
    security, material possessions,
or their own family's needs the focus of their lives
and are now discovering the futility and emptiness
    it brings.
Ask that Christ's coming may open their eyes to
    see life through God's eyes.

Think of a world leader facing huge decisions in
    the midst of complex choices.
Think of a nation weakened by years of indulgence
    and selfish living.
Think of a society reaping the harvest of the seeds
    of permissiveness and immorality.
Ask that the promise of Christ's coming again may
    turn their hearts and minds to their Maker.

Think of yourself and all your life means.
Think of all you possess and all you have done.
Think of all it will mean in the face of eternity and
    think of your relationship now with your God.

Think of all you will face tomorrow
and ask that Christ's coming and coming again will
    focus you daily on him.

In the name of Christ, who came and is coming.
Amen.

ALWAYS THE SAME

Lord, you are always the same, always coming,
    ever present.
We pray for those who feel lost and alone;
for those who even in a crowd have a sense
    of isolation.
We pray for those who have failed
and for those whose sense of failure is false
and for all who need to know the hand of God
    upon their lives again.
Lord, in your mercy,
hear our prayer.

Lord, you are always the same, always coming,
    ever present.
We pray for those who feel overwhelmed by life;
by the decisions they must make and by situations
over which they seem to have so little control.
We pray for those defeated by life or by illness
or by the constant strain of caring for family or friends.
May the rich love of God supply their needs.

Lord, in your mercy,
hear our prayer.

Lord, you are always the same, always coming,
ever present.
We pray for those whose memories haunt them and
hurt them;
for those who are abused and for those rejected by
family and friends.
We pray for those whose choices are limited by
their poverty
and their lives by the domination of others.
We pray for those imprisoned by guilt or despair,
by anxiety or disability.
May the love of God hold, heal, and set them free.
Lord, in your mercy,
hear our prayer.

Lord, you are always the same, always coming,
ever present.
We pray for those who feel as if they do not matter,
those who are not valued, those whose gifts and
talents are no longer needed.
We pray for those who have nowhere to call home,
those who sleep rough, those who lack the ability
to cope,
and those who refuse to try.
May the gentle love of God guide them in ways
that are new.

Lord, in your mercy,
hear our prayer.

Lord, you are always the same, always coming,
    ever present.
We pray for ourselves who, like Mary, are always
    surprised
to learn that you have given us a place in your kingdom
and that you can use even us in your service.
Keep our ears and eyes open, we pray,
ready to say yes when you call,
open to your Holy Spirit's power to enable us
    to respond.
Lord, in your mercy,
hear our prayer.

Lord, you are always the same, always coming,
    ever present,
always coming again.
Hear our prayers, and, by your Holy Spirit,
use us as a means of answering them. **Amen.**

HELP US TO SEE

Father, when we see a lost and troubled world,
and when we are aware of the sadness, sorrow, and
    pain all around us,
we pray, send your word of hope, love, and joy
to bring an end to guilt and fear and suffering.

Lord, you see everything;
come, come open our eyes.

Father, open our eyes that, like the prophets of old,
we may become more aware of your glory
and your power surrounding us on every side.
We pray, save us from despair, fill us with courage,
join our wills to yours, and make us channels of
   your grace
and messengers of your word in all we say and
   do and are.
Lord, you see everything;
come, come open our eyes.

Father, we pray for your church when we lose our way
and are in danger of losing our hold on you.
Give us faith to believe, hope to reach out, and love
   to make real.
Rekindle our faith in the promises given to us in
   the Bible,
that all tears will be wiped away as death, sadness,
   crying, and pain
will cease through the power of your word in Christ.
Lord, you see everything;
come, come open our eyes.

Father, we pray for Christians everywhere,
that they might have the courage to stand firm
on the promises and teaching of Scripture.

In a world that increasingly turns its back on its Maker,
keep all your people faithful to you and your Word.
Give us the courage, the power, and the conviction
not only to live by your Word
but to make it known everywhere and to everyone.
Lord, you see everything;
come, come open our eyes.

Father, we pray for all who are abused, ignored,
or made to feel as if they do not matter.
Wherever there is hurt and pain,
may there be the word of healing;
where there is cruelty, violence, and oppression,
may there be your word of hope;
where there is injustice, brokenness, and arrogance,
may there be your word of peace.
Lord, you see everything;
come, come open our eyes.

Father, we pray for ourselves
as you continue to convince us of your
tremendous power.
Assure us of the height, depth, length, and
breadth of your love.
By your Holy Spirit, save us from despair,
fill us with your power, and be present with
us and for us for ever.
Lord, you see everything;
come, come open our eyes.

In the name of Christ,
God's word to a lost and hurting world. **Amen.**

FOR ORDINARY PEOPLE

Father, we pray for ourselves and Christians
    everywhere,
that we may have a clear vision
of your purpose for our lives and the life of
    your church.
May we have the courage, strength, and
    determination
to allow nothing and no one to deflect us from it.
The Lord hears our prayer.
Thanks be to God.

We pray for quiet Christians;
those whose names will never hit the headlines,
whose personalities are not dynamic
and who know they may never set the
    world on fire;
for Christians who faithfully serve in the
    background,
that they may know that nothing they do in
    his service is ever wasted
and that its value is measured only by the
    love of Christ.
The Lord hears our prayer.
Thanks be to God.

We pray for all whose daily care, compassion, and
understanding
prepare the hearts and minds of those they meet
at home, at work, at school, or in the world for the
coming of Christ;
and for those whose words and deeds
enable others to be open to God's words for them
in Jesus.
The Lord hears our prayer.
Thanks be to God.

We pray, restore our confidence in you
to change lives and transform every situation
and to move nations through the power
of the Holy Spirit;
for Christians in positions where they can bring
your influence to bear upon the life of society;
for those who teach or lead young people;
for those who work in the advertising industry;
for those who work in radio or television;
for leaders of nations, preachers of the gospel,
and pastors and parents.
The Lord hears our prayer.
Thanks be to God.

We pray, help us, weak as we are,
to go to those overwhelmed by grief, broken
by violence,

crushed by injustice, damaged by abuse,
    weakened by illness.
Lord, fill us with the Holy Spirit that we
    may take with us
the power to heal and transform.
The Lord hears our prayer.
Thanks be to God.

We pray for ourselves, that you will move again
    within our hearts and lives
that we may be aware again of your still, small voice.
Lord, call us by name, commission us to serve, heal
    our wounds, renew our lives.
Lord, when we feel lost, empty, and alone,
may your presence find us, fill us,
comfort us, and enable us to stand
    and to go on standing.
The Lord hears our prayer.
Thanks be to God.

In the name of him who came, comes,
and goes on coming, Christ the Lord. **Amen.**

PRAYERS OF COMMITMENT

WE BELONG

Help us, Father, as those who belong to your Son,
to fulfil our commitment to you and to one another.
Help us to leave behind all that hinders our walk
    with Christ
and enable us, by your Spirit,
to love our neighbour as ourselves and honour
    Christ as Lord. **Amen.**

RENEWING OUR HOPE

Lord, in Jesus Christ you have brought us into
    your church
so that we might claim the world again for you.
Keep renewing our hope and faith, forgiving our sin,
    increasing our praise
so that your name will be glorified in us as it
    has been,

and always will be, in Christ our Saviour and Lord.
Amen.

WE CAN GO

We can go because he came.
We can be sent because he goes with us.
We can stand because he is Lord.
We can do all things in Christ
who gives us the strength. **Amen.**

WE CAN COME

Lord, we come to you because in Christ you first
came to us.
We open our lives to you because Christ has poured
out his life for us.
We commit ourselves to you
because in Christ you demonstrated your eternal
commitment to us. **Amen.**

PRAYERS FOR DISMISSAL

AS SURELY

As surely as the Lord came,
as surely as he will come again,
so you can be sure that he is with you
    and you with him,
and so it will be for ever. **Amen.**

GO NOW

Go now, the world is waiting.
Go now, God gives us the power.
Go now, for he is with us.
Go now, for now is the time to go!

NO MATTER

No matter who you are or what you have done;
no matter where you are or what you are facing;

no matter how you feel or whether you understand it;
the truth is this: you can go in hope, joy, and peace,
for Christ has come! **Amen.**

HAVE NO FEAR

Have no fear.
He is Lord and he is with you and will walk with you,
talk with you, and be in you and you in him, always.
Amen.

ABOUT THE AUTHOR

David Clowes, born in Ellesmere Port, left school at fifteen following a secondary modern education. In 1965 he committed his life to Christ at Heaton Mersey Methodist and in 1967 he received God's call into the Methodist ministry. He trained at Hartley Victoria College and gained a degree in theology at the University of Manchester.

David served in a number of churches in the northwest of England before retiring in 2010 after thirty-five years in active ministry. His first book, *500 Prayers for All Occasions*, began as a spiritual exercise during a sabbatical. This was followed by *500 More Prayers for All Occasions*. His third book of prayers, *500 Prayers for the Christian Year*, is based on scriptures from the Revised Common Lectionary.

David is married to Angela, and they have two married sons, a foster son, and four grandchildren.